Real Torn…
Beneath the Veil

Pamela L. Ellis

PublishAmerica
Baltimore

© 2007 by Pamela L. Ellis.
All rights reserved. No part of this book may be reproduced, stored in a retrieval system or transmitted in any form or by any means without the prior written permission of the publishers, except by a reviewer who may quote brief passages in a review to be printed in a newspaper, magazine or journal.

First printing

Unless otherwise indicated, Bible quotations are taken from King James Version of the Bible. Copyright © 2007 to be published by PublishAmerica.

ISBN: 1-4241-9430-X
PUBLISHED BY PUBLISHAMERICA, LLLP
www.publishamerica.com
Baltimore

Printed in the United States of America

I dedicate this book to my grandfather, Harry Bradley, who is now deceased. He was saved, sanctified, filled with the Holy Ghost, and told me about God at the young age of five. I am thankful that he instructed me as a child in the way that I should go; as a result, I am fully-grown and it shall not depart.

Train up a child in the way they should go and when they are full-grown it shall not depart (Proverbs 22:6).

Introduction

The Lord God has given me the tongue of the learned, that I should know how to speak, a word in season to him who is weary. He awakens me morning by morning, He awakens my ear to hear as the learned (Isaiah 50:4).

Real Torn

No one could get under my skin, beneath the hurt, pacify the pain or fix the problem. I was held back from moving forward, knocked down each time that I stood, and I endured decades of torment. Not enough to kill but just enough to keep me real torn, only Jesus could take what was broken and mend it back together again.

Table of Contents

Summary	11
The Destroyer	11
Preface	13
At Five	13
At Ten	14
At Thirteen	15
Chapter One	17
Sixteen	17
Self-Esteem	18
The Pain	19
Chapter Two	20
The Cover-Up	20
The Cover-Up: Two	21
The Cover-Up, Too	22
Chapter Three	23
The Struggle	23
The People	24
On the Journey	25
Chapter Four	26
The Cost	26
Reality	27
Twenty-Six Years	28

Chapter Five — 30
   The Facts — 30
   The Deliverance — 31
   The Growth — 32

Chapter Six — 34
   The Breakthrough — 34
   I'm Free — 35
   My Father's Business — 36

Chapter Seven — 38
   At Forty-Two — 38
   New Beginnings — 39
   The Work — 40

P.A.S.S.I.O.N: — 42
Power & Atonement for Suffering, Sin, and Iniquities in Our Nation/
Monthly Sermons for Daily Life

Works Cited — 56

Biography — 59

Summary

The Destroyer

 The thief comes but to kill, steal, and destroy (John 10:10). At the age of four, the devil began to set me up. He destroyed my beauty and kept me broken, that he might keep me down. He crushed my need to be loved that I might not love others. The devil knew that if I ever got a revelation of who Jesus was, I'd be dangerous, so he started early to ruin me. That devil knew that if I ever found out that I am more than a conqueror through Christ Jesus, I would be dynamic. So he set a trap, a trap that would ensnare me for a very long time, it wasn't enough to kill me, but enough to hold me bound for a while. He caused me to believe that I would never be the same, my problem was bigger, and I would never get better. Satan attacked me at my weakest point; I was helpless and felt terribly unworthy. He is the father of lies and a thief; your adversary the devil walks about as a roaring lion seeking whom he may devour (I Peter 5:8). That thief knew that he had to get up early in the morning and never sleep to keep me depressed. That liar set me up to destroy everything that I should've been. He stole my precious moments, my security and my identity; that devil made me sick. He kept me depressed, distressed and emotionally oppressed, I couldn't think straight, walk right, or focus on anything except my problems. He destroyed my self-esteem and attempted to keep me scorned over the years. He showed me that he is the recruiter leading people into the cares of this world and eventually to hell, for he knows that his time is coming. Now I have power to tread on scorpions and servants and over all the power of the enemy, and nothing shall by any means hurt me (Luke 10:19). Jesus said, "Don't rejoice that I have power over the devil, but that my name is written in the Lamb's Book of Life," (Luke 10:20). The devil thought he had me, for life.

Preface

At Five

My grandfather took all of the grandkids to church every Sunday; afterwards, he took us to Red Barns, McDonald's, or Top Hats to eat. He put so much money in the tray that I didn't think he'd have anything left for our meals (it was at least nine of us). One day, I was on my brother's back and fell down on the concrete basement floor. I burst my forehead right in the middle. Okay, I didn't know at the time that I was supposed to be cute. A few years later I went to grade school; no real problem, I don't remember anyone mocking me. Life was simple and very much normal. We were kids. I wasn't aware of the beauties that glamorized the world. At five, I had a mind of a child, so I thought like a child and did childish things. It wasn't until I was fully grown that I thought like an adult, and experienced all of an adult's pain, troubles, and faults. My mother took me to the hospital (I remember lying on that bed), in what I assumed to be the morning hours because she had to wait for my uncle to get home with my grandmothers' car. Life was real simple, no real tragedies that I could see at the time. If there was a problem in store for my future, it was unknown to me. Time went on, we moved on, I wasn't hurt and really didn't care. My mother was mad about my forehead, and I believe she nurtured me the best way that she knew to do. My brother told me he was sorry and that was it. Oh, I got a sucker from the doctor that stitched my forehead together. A permanent scar, I should have planned on wearing this for a long time, until around the time of death. Might as well get used to it; there was nothing I could do—no use in crying over spilled milk. It didn't matter, I was the same old kid—playing, getting dirty, and waiting to do it all again the next day. I didn't have any problems so I didn't make up one. I continued to go to church with my granddad, in Sunday school every Sunday, I was well on my way.

PAMELA L. ELLIS

At Ten

There was a woman in the neighbor name Sister Chapman. Everyone went to her house; we had what I now know to be a revival. She led everybody to Jesus; I saw so many older adults praying, crying and praising the Lord. People loved this woman, me especially, because she loved everybody with such genuineness. Her husband was so mean. I remember him drinking while we were there, but he didn't mess with us. Now I know that the Holy Ghost had him under control; he couldn't mess with us. After saying the sinner's prayer I was saved, but didn't have a relationship with Jesus. I didn't know that I could talk to Him, He to me, and expect results. I went over to Sister Chapman's house a few more times and quit. We moved away, I believe. When I did go over there she had moved. Well there goes my first spiritual leader; I didn't know it then. My God, I had no idea that I was headed for some mess in my life. I was too young to understand all of that stuff—spiritual warfare in high places, what did it mean, what was it for.... I wish she could have been around longer to help me get through some stuff. Just thinking about her in my mind, I still remember her glowing face. She had the Lord written all over her face—wow, such an awesome demonstration of His power. Maybe she was there only for a season to win souls to Christ; whatever her reasons, I was glad that I met her. When Sister Chapman left the neighborhood, almost every one backslid and went into their same old business. There was no one to come in her place, at least I didn't hear about it. That devil knew that I would see my potential; so he tried to destroy me once again. My grandfather continued to take us to church, but when I was thirteen he died in a house fire trying to save my younger cousins. I couldn't understand why God let my grandfather die in that fire (he was saved, sanctified and filled with the Holy Ghost). It wasn't until I was older and back in the Lord that I understood; God would never leave him or forsake him. He met my granddad in the mist of that fire, held out his hand and called him home. I believe that with all the power that the Lord has invested in me.

At Thirteen

My grandfather had passed away, so I would go to church with the next-door neighbors, sometimes. This same neighbor had a dog in their yard that barked and growled all the time. I wasn't afraid because the dog always remained tied to the pole. On one day in particular, I took the garbage to the alley and told the dog to shut up (may have even growled back at him). Unfortunately, the dog broke the chain, he jumped on my side of the yard, and I jumped on his side. He caught me on his side of the yard holding on to his pole. I stood screaming as I watched this dog chew my right leg as if it were a piece of meat; the devil had a trap set. From that moment forward I didn't wear a pair of shorts without socks to cover my wounds. Growing older I continued to cover my leg, I was so embarrassed about it. I would wear one sock down to show my pretty leg, and the other sock up to cover my horrible leg. As if one of my socks fell down all by itself, I would leave it that way all the day long. Most children pulled both knee socks up. Not me. I was always hiding, and very skeptical about wearing shorts. Hot summer days would come and pass over me as if to scorn me. I couldn't enjoy the season because I had to overdress; no shorts, no sundress, no peace, and certainly no happiness. Why do things always have to happen to me? What's the matter with me that I always get the repercussion of someone else's error? Why was this happening to me now? What had I done to deserve this? I was just a kid, a kid who hadn't had an opportunity to become someone, still dependent on my mother. My life hadn't even started. I was still wet behind the ears, and here I was experiencing the type of pain that grown-ups cry about. We didn't have money; therefore, surgery was out of the question. The owners of the dog paid the doctor's bill and gave him to the dog pound to be euthanized.

Chapter One

Sixteen

    At sixteen, my life was really getting started. I was trying to put the past behind me and move on to better things. That devil wasn't through; I was struck in the face with a drinking glass while attending school. That incident left three more scars on my face. Now I have three on the forehead and one on the bridge of my nose. The most sensitive part of my life was the scars inflicted on my face. The mere thought of going through life like this devastated me. This is a real sensitive issue. I was not a kid anymore, it was not all right, I was older now, and looks did matter. I wanted to fall dead I was hopeless just bury me. I let my problems take over me; I started to give up on everything, I didn't care. No one felt my pain or knew what they would do if it was their problem, nor did they care. To tell you the truth, there was only one who cared and knew my deepest darkest secret; little did I know him, yet. I didn't know that He was there each time that I cried at night. He was there when I hated myself and didn't see a reason for living. I got saved, but didn't have a relationship with Him; no one explained it that way. I said, "I'll never marry, never have children, never amount to anything. I'm doomed." How could I overcome, what must I do? It wasn't that I thought that I was so cute (not that I was so ugly either), I simply wasn't aware of that possibility. It never entered my mind that I was cute like other girls; after all, I was never told. Oh well, at sixteen that didn't matter to me anyway, I was only trying to find my purpose in life. At that age, it's prime time, going to school, expecting things to get better and better, not from worse to worse. I wasn't aware that I'd experience a change in life that would affect my self-esteem, self-worth, inner being, and my ability to be all that God made me to be. There were certain ways that I could hide my secret from others, but not from myself. I had no idea that I was about to be challenged for the next 26 years of my life, only to become bitter, broken, and very lost—happy one moment, and sad the next. Why did I have to suffer? I was a good person that treated everyone nice; I never tried to abuse anyone. Why do bad things happen to good people? Seems like all the good people die first and suffer more. What's wrong with this scenario? "Help!"

Self-Esteem

Self-esteem is the amount of confidence a person has for themselves. I had low self-esteem I wasn't confident at all, it took a lot to be me. I had no real character. I once heard Bishop T.D. Jakes say, "A low-grade version of a deeply saddened girl." That was me growing up to be a miserable woman. I didn't know that I would be called of God; I had no idea of the tremendous change predestined in years to come. For now, this girl was wounded beyond measure; I lived for hope—never wanting much, just a normal life. To be beautiful like other people, to belong to something or someone that loved me. I needed to be wanted, to have the opportunity that Cinderella had—not in a fairytale state, but a real life situation. I've dreamed and fantasized of this moment for me, a gorgeous woman who keeps herself for the perfect husband. This woman was not only beautiful outside, but her spirit was full of love and happiness. She was a magnificent creation of what a man looked for in a woman. I was so messed up; I could never be that person. I could never live the life of a person with such character. As I looked at the mirror once more I cried out in despair. I knew that over the course of my life, I would look into a mirror an amount of times that is impossible to calculate. I wanted to see these scars, look at them and wonder how could I hide them today. I couldn't look at the mirror and say, "Look how cute you are. Girl, you are so fine." Not me, it was hopeless. I was stricken by a scar that nobody but Jesus could heal. Why didn't I give it to him and leave it there? Why did I take it back? What was so difficult about crying, handing it over, and leaving it alone? What was my real problem, why couldn't I get through this thing? All those emotions ran through my mind. It's a wonder I'm still here; I should have died long time ago with all that mess in my head.

The Pain

There was always the pressure of trying to prepare myself to fit in society. Most people groom themselves and go on about their business. Not me; I had to go the extra mile. I wanted to be accepted, I certainly didn't want to be rejected or laughed at. This was my problem, my pain, and my struggle. I had the right to disguise myself the way that I wanted to, or did I? Was it that necessary for me to pay close attention to myself? In a way, I inflicted my own afflictions; I was my worst nightmare. As the years went by, I remained frustrated beyond measure and angry at the world. My whole life was turned upside down; most times I would simply stay in the house. When I did go out, I wore a headband everywhere that I went. If I dressed formally, I would cut something, anything that would match my outfit—real broken, real pain. If I couldn't find a headband to match my outfit, I would tear a piece of the material off of what I had on. If I couldn't tear a piece of the hem, I'd change my whole outfit. I was messed up. Although everyone became accustomed to me wearing the headbands, I was still the talk of the party. I assume people used to wonder, *Why does she have that headband on again, what is really her problem?* I used to wash my hair with the headband on, take a shower with that headband on. People must have thought that I was crazy. I wasn't, just torn, real torn. A thought remained in the back of my mind, *Everyone takes an educated guess, that when I walk into the room or come outside, I would have on a headband.* I spent a couple of decades of my life in a serious mental state, with issues that I couldn't or wouldn't overcome. I had a secret that I didn't show to my best friend, a secret that I didn't want my mother to see, and a real tragedy. How could I ever get over this thing? How could I ever get free from my misery? I used to wonder how did I get so far away from myself, why didn't I pay more attention to me. How come it never dawned on me that I am somebody? Nevertheless, it didn't matter, and from the looks of my face it never would.

Chapter Two

The Cover-Up

    Bitterly, I continued to wear headbands throughout my teenage/young adult years. That was the method that I used to hide the scars so that I could get from point A to B. To get a job, go to work, activity time, socializing, the headband was my life. There were secrets on my forehead that I couldn't let anyone see, partly for fear of what people may say, but mainly to hide from myself that the scars were permanently visible. After I realized that the styles were changing, I couldn't wear the headbands any longer. *Oh no, what will I do now?* I wanted to fall out and die. I didn't know what to do; as a result, I went outside with a stocking cap on pretending that I had permed my hair, or a shower cap as if I just finished washing my hair. It was terrible. I made certain that the caps were pulled down over my forehead; remember I couldn't let anyone see my secret. I would say things like, "My hair isn't completely dry." After awhile, people must have wondered, *Why does she still have that cap on? Come on now, the day is over; it's almost nighttime.* Okay, I was lying, and had to tell another lie to cover that one. I was not proud of lying; it wasn't my intent. "HELP!" I needed Jesus, personally. At twenty-five years old I grew tired of the bands; after all, they were with me wherever I went ever since I were sixteen. God was working on me then, but I missed it. Instead of me taking that sign of weariness and throwing the bands away, I had to think of something different, but what? The biggest scar is on the bridge of my nose right between my eyes. Although I wore the headband to cover the scars on my forehead, there was none to cover the bridge of my nose. I guess I should've been thankful that I wasn't blinded by the impact; I thought I was thankful. Or, was I so wrapped up in despair that I couldn't see the blessing of having my eyesight? Lord forgive me; I didn't know how to be grateful for the little things because I was worrying about the bigger thing, or visa versa.

The Cover-Up: Two

As time went on, I had to think of an idea to conceal my forehead without the headbands. "Eureka!" I had an idea. I could take the relaxing gel and flatten my hair down on my forehead. It was magnificent, I thought. I'd put just enough gel on my hair, and slick my bangs down right on top of the scars. Now I could go outside like anyone else, without a care in the world. Sometimes the gel would dry out, and instead of my bang sticking to my forehead, it would come loose. I thought that I would come unglued the first time that it happened. I was outside, probably a long way from home, and in front of many people. I remember the embarrassment, thinking, *Oh my, what if the wind blow and make my bangs come up.* I thought, *I have to go out and buy a more expensive gel, and put a double layer on.* People could see the scars on the bridge of my nose, but if they ever saw all of the scars at once, I would shrink, literally. I would rather die. If that wind blew I would quickly run for cover. Overall, the hairstyle allowed me to laugh again, and to be a part of all the festivities that took place in life. I was almost vain, had more confidence, and knew I looked good—even thought that I was sexy. I had a new way of saying look world, I'm cute too. I said to myself again, "They can't see my forehead, but they can see the scar on the bridge of my nose." The devil had a trap set; I thought that I looked good, but I was sinking back into the hole that I climbed out of. Oh it was devastating, but I had to get over it. I had to live; besides, what else could I do. After all, I have to go out into the world, go to clubs, and make a grand entrance into the roller-skating rink where all the boys were. I was young—outside world, here I come. The outside world had its ups and downs, setbacks and turnarounds, but I was out there in it, alienated from God, not to mention I'd completely forgotten about being saved. I had a new love—me; after all, the new look meant the world to me, and I had suffered a long time. I couldn't see Jesus; I had to pay close attention to me. I was so excited, free from the bands and proud of my new look, very pleased. I wasn't aware that pride goes before a fall (Proverbs 16:18). God was not pleased, and the devil had a trap set. I was set up for the fall. Once I took my eyes off of the Lord, the agreement was signed, and still I didn't know that I would be scorned for the next twenty-six years of my life.

PAMELA L. ELLIS

The Cover-Up, Too

    Going out I had to put the final touch on my hair, to be certain that everything was in place. I had a reputation to fulfill; I couldn't be a laughing stock. I was trying to uphold my image. What image, what am I thinking, what had come over me, and what have I become? What did all of this have to do with me being a human being, a child of God? Why is it that I feel the need to cover my true identity only to settle for a fake one? I was kidding myself with another fantasy; I need to get real, but not now. What a pity, a set up, and a cover up, to destroy me. Sent by the tragedy thief, the devil, it was all arranged to break me. Lord I really missed it; I wanted to belong, to be cute and to be accepted; regrettably, I forgot about You in the midst of my hurt. Unfortunately, it was hard for me to try to work on myself, praise you, and feel good. The gel started to get messy; in the summer the heat made the gel run down my face, my neck, and right onto my clothes. Time for another cover up so soon; I was sick and tired of being sick and tired. There was no rest for me; on my left and on my right was nothing but heartache. Bitterness began to sink in again, I felt myself sinking back into the whole, but this time placing a lid on top after me. The time had come for me to make an intelligent decision; I couldn't wear this gel any longer. Okay, I let the gel go and replaced it with my bangs; this was scary for me because I didn't know the outcome. I knew that people wore bangs and when they wanted to change their hair-do they did. I went through a decade and a half wearing bangs; there weren't many ways that I could wear my hair. Tortured, distraught, and very much depressed, I was torn up, futile. I stood in my tracks staring at the scars and couldn't help but notice the tears. At times I would cry uncontrollably; the pressure was real. I was damaged for life. Couldn't God see my pain; didn't He recognize that I was in deep agony? The Bible says that He won't give us more than we can handle. Didn't He realize that this was more than I could handle?

Chapter Three

The Struggle

    I tried to fix it; I tried to hold my head up. I pretended (did it well) that everything was okay. I hid who I was in order to be beautiful on the outside; it didn't matter that I was torn on the inside. I didn't understand that my life had this sudden turn for my good, lest I think more highly of myself (Romans 12:3). Come on, I didn't have a clue what that meant at the time, I didn't know how to walk in faith. I had no real relationship with Jesus. I didn't care about the reasons; there was no reason for me to look this way, only sorrow. Seemed like sorrow that lasted forever, nothing else mattered; how could I move on? Every time someone spoke to me I had to give some form of eye contact. Sometimes I would hold my head down while talking, pretending that I had lost something, looking for something, or just had plain old low self esteem (no eye contact whatsoever). A glance at a time was appropriate; after all, I couldn't be rude all the time. Oh God, why couldn't these scars be on another part of my body? Why my face? What a nightmare, a roller-coaster ride, a tragedy that happened to a sixteen-year-old girl who didn't have a beginning, and certainly not an end. Broken, bitter, and very lost. It was a tragedy, and I was bound by the circumstances of life. Reluctant to grow and refusing to trust in the only one that could walk me through this struggle, this heartache, and the demon that was sent to destroy me. Jesus would have saved me from my dilemma if only I knew then what I know now. I used to fix a bang in the front of my hairline all the time; don't let the wind blow. I didn't care who was there. I would act cold or something (to play it off), and look the other way so that the wind wouldn't blow my bangs and reveal my scars. Just as long as my bangs were in place, I was fine. I could enjoy the day somewhat, but I was always on the edge of my seat, ready to dart for cover if the wind should blow. A tragedy. It was almost funny, but sad, real sad.

The People

What could friends have said, what suggestions would've been deemed appropriate? How did people perceive me? It mattered to me what people thought. I couldn't get past what people said about me; it became one of my major concerns. Everyone knew me, they didn't all like me and I may have not liked all of them, but we knew each other. At any rate, I was so concerned with what people thought, as if they cared enough to see about me. I recall this woman saying to me, "People will hurt you." I had to redirect my thinking. I didn't know at the time that people couldn't handle their own problems; therefore, I didn't realize that I shouldn't be concerned about what they thought about mine. I wanted to be loved, for someone to check on me. I cared for attention. I was alone a lot, but okay with it. I never wanted to be around many folks because of my issue, but I cared about people and loved real hard. I used to give all that I had even my last, I'd promise to do, or do it for you. Only to find out that although I had given all of myself, it didn't make anyone like me more. It didn't necessarily make them like me any less, but certainly not more. I guess that I expected to gain some type of repayment or replacement in exchange for my loss. I expected people to love me as I loved them, I expected too much. I had to realize that people are just people and it wasn't fair for me to hold someone accountable for my happiness. My happiness is not in someone else's head and it wasn't up to people to fulfill me, but up to me. As I got older, life began to take a different turn; people didn't want to be bothered with other people's problems. I couldn't blame them, I lived with a lot of people. You name it, wherever I could stay. Some people took advantage of me because I was weak, had no place to go, and no place to hide. I responded by doing what I was told, followed some instructions, and continued to hold onto the misery that I hid deep down inside. I had to compromise to stay where I didn't want to be; there was no other choice. I had two problems, the one that I was given to bury with, and the one that was given to me by others. The years that I spent being taken advantage of, used, and mistreated (I was insecure). I told myself again and again that I could get through this dilemma and go on with my life. I wrestled with the pressure and endured the pain; some of the situations could have been avoided, but the devil had a trap set. Except God ultimately brought me out. What was He saving me for? Why did He stay for the long haul? Back then I didn't have a clue.

On the Journey

    Despair is such a difficult emotion to grasp; the torment, grief, and an insurmountable burden kept me lingering in the past. Through the years I hadn't gained any real rewards because I had not trained myself. This was my problem. I could pamper it any way that I wanted. I supported my feelings by giving it reason to hold on to the pain. I came from bad to worse, worse to worst and got worse. I became bitter and grew tired of wearing my hair in a certain way to cover my forehead. At this point, I let the problem take over me. I said, "I don't care any more," not enough to let anyone see, but just enough to let myself go. I started to tell myself, "This is it, I give up, and I won't amount to anything," just like others had said. My life had no purpose, no real meaning, and I didn't care about myself (only for others). I was introduced to drugs and alcohol at age nineteen, to be exact. The introduction that turned me away from the Lord; oh the devil had a trap set. I was in the world and doing things that I had no business doing. I guess that I still loved the Lord, but wasn't doing what He told me to do. Happy one moment but sad the next, rejoicing one day and crying the next, I didn't want to talk to a psychiatrist. I wasn't crazy just depressed. I was in need of the original surgeon, Jesus; I had a need but couldn't reach it alone. I began to look at the lives of others and noticed that there were a lot of backbitten evildoers, with great lives and cute faces. I thought, *How could people be so wicked and have every need met?* Now I know that God wrote a book of remembrance. Then you shall again discern between the righteous and the wicked, between one who serves God and one who does not serve Him (Malachi 3:18). I'm glad that I saw that scripture, it was necessary for me, because I was devastated thinking that the wicked always overcame, and that they never had any problems or a worry. I thought that their lives were perfect and that the saved just kept enduring never-ending pain. Despair will make you think a lot of things that aren't true.

Chapter Four

The Cost

Situations that arise in life are always costly. It isn't always monetary but everything is associated with a price. The cost of living, the cost of marriage, and the cost of child bearing are all traditional costs. The cost of being saved is costly because the anointing of God costs much. We may try to weigh our problems and decide which one is lighter than the other; nevertheless, they're all about the same rate—it's costly. You may have to get rid of some stuff, some of that mess you've been holding onto. You may have to give up some of those unsaved friends, pray and love them from a distance. If your spouse isn't acting right, it may have an additional cost, which may be too expensive to afford. The price that I had to pay for misfortune, sadness and shame was a lot. It cost me everything that I had, and everyone that I came in contact with was affected. It cost them because I never gave anyone all that they were to receive from me. I couldn't be all that I was supposed to be, all that God made me, or touch those that I came in contact with. Under the circumstances, I was reluctant, maybe even terrified of being all that God made me to be. Therefore, I cheated my family, friends, and enemies out of all that they were to gather from me. At that time, I had not expected to be responsible for the well being of others. I didn't know that people learned and gained experience from other people, and that my tragedy may have helped someone else. After all, I was crushed, in my eyes destroyed, written off as someone who wouldn't amount to anything. I was hurt, very angry and fell into a deep depression. Often I would wonder why I had to have these scars; I lacked in most efforts of ever becoming successful. The willingness was gone, the purpose wasn't there, and the need couldn't be found. The real answer to these trials may never be known, and I may wonder for the rest of my life. In my mind if I could pick one thing, it wouldn't be to go around this mountain again, but to know how to climb over it. We as people are not always eager to pay the full price; we would rather get the bargain—not knowing that the name brand lasts longer; thus, that is the reason that it cost a little bit more. What we go through is truly worth it for the kingdom of God, whatever the charge. It cost me a fortune, but the truth has to be told, I had to go through something to get to where God wanted me to be.

Reality

It was hard to face reality, even harder when reality hits you in the face (I was hit in the face, literally). Some people are in the same category, but just a few. I want to challenge you—what would you do, surgery? I thought about it but didn't have the money for it; besides, it may have left a different scar. Just thinking about a new face made me uncomfortable, brand new scars could be devastating to the breaking point of suicide. I got that thought out my mind as soon as it entered, quickly replacing it with another, as I focused continually on the next. I couldn't believe that the scars didn't go away last night. I couldn't imagine going through the rest of my life this way. I needed help, I needed support; someone help me, please. The reality finally sunk in that there was no one that could help. There was no one coming to take my pain and no one that could hear my plea. As a result, I became accustomed to a different type of struggle. Remember I mentioned the cost; everything is associated with a cost. I went out into the world to try and pacify my pain. I straddled the fence (there was no way that God would honor that). It didn't work; it cost me more to go out there, and hurt me just as much to give up the safety of God's arms. I missed the compassion that God showed through His grace and love towards me. Going back to the glitter of the world, (everything that glitters isn't gold), and the next thing that I knew I was in court paying fines and monthly fees. I had taken a turn that I would soon regret, but it was a wake-up call for me to let go of all that kept me bound. The scars, the parties, the drinking, and smoking— I had to stop making these things my lord. It pacified the pain only for a while, and then it closed the door with me inside, trapped. It wasn't easy, but I had to give back to the Lord what was already His— me. My problems were not my own, I had to go to the Father and tell Him what the devil stole from me. I held up my own blessings, I caused my own setbacks; I had help though, the devil made it his business to keep me down. Finally, I had come again face to face with reality; I didn't need the devil to supply me with anything, no more traps. My God shall supply all my needs according to His riches in glory by Christ Jesus (Philippians 4:19).

Twenty-Six Years

No wonder the devil set a trap for me; he tried to destroy me as a child so that I wouldn't be a mouthpiece for Jesus (I've got a big mouth). Use me, Lord. Sadly, I gave up on most of my dreams in which I could have become. I didn't have any interest; I was stricken with a problem that wouldn't go away. As I looked in the mirror again, day after day, I became more and more frustrated at what stared back at me. My problem stuck with me, I was never all that I could be, and now, I certainly never would be. I didn't enjoy my teenage years because I was so unhappy. I remained secluded from most of the events that teenagers did. The only thing that I could become a professional in was roller-skating (it was normal to wear headbands at the rink). Set back from enjoying my life, set back from going to school, set back from being all that God made me to be. I didn't have the motivation to carry on; the willingness to *do* was gone. I didn't want to become anything; the mountain was too high to climb, and the road too long to walk. Always sitting, always waiting, but what was I waiting for, a miracle? I guess it took so long for my breakthrough because I believed some things some of the time. I believed the word of God, but I didn't listen carefully to what He was saying to me. I didn't react on what He told me that I was to Him. He said, "Trust Me, I will help you. Don't worry." I heard it, and I said, "Thank you, Jesus," but I didn't apply it to my situation. I had to get an understanding of what the word said. It took a while for me, but may not take a while for you. Twenty-six years is a long time to be stagnant, and stuck. I should have been dead and sleeping in my grave. But God said, "I wish that none will perish and that all will come into the knowledge of the truth" (2 Peter 3:9). For all of those years I believed a lie, I believed that I would never amount to anything. I believed that I was mentally scarred for life. I believed that I was ugly, but little did I know that there are some of the ugliest cute people. Cute on the outside, but all messed up in the heart, which makes the outside appearance unattractive as well. God looks on the heart, I am so glad that my heart was okay. It was sad that my face was ugly but my heart wasn't. Maybe some of you have been cute all your life; I didn't have that privilege, but now I am not ashamed. I was angry about what happen to me in my life, but I always had a heart for people. Now I've been called to help them.

Chapter Five

The Facts

I didn't have a relationship with Jesus at first. I was saved because I believed that He died on the cross for my sins, and God raised Him from the dead on the third day (Romans 10:9). I was saved, but in order for me to gain control over the little things, I had to know in my knower that Jesus had set me free. I had to stand on the promises of His word, and apply them to my life. Jesus did it all when He died on Calvary, thank God for Jesus. If it had not been for Jesus, I would have been dead and sleeping in my grave. I had to grab hold of what I believed. It was time to stand on the promises; time to do what God said I could do. The Holy Ghost spoke to me and said, "You got to get rid of some stuff." I had to make Jesus my Lord, and give him my situation, my circumstance and my problems. I had to give Him my pain and my pressure. It wasn't easy to do, no it wasn't, but once I believed what God told me, about me, I was able to give up a lot of things. I had to fix my way of thinking, to think about what God said to nobody but me. If God hasn't spoken to you yet, He will. Jesus said, "Ask, and it shall be given to you. Seek, and you shall find. Knock, and the door will be opened to you" (Matthew 7:7). Just as you have a relationship with your parents, siblings, and friends you must have that first and foremost relationship with the Lord. I couldn't fight the battle alone. I had to build up my faith; I had to have help. I needed help, the kind that only God can give; it starts from above. There is a way of escape for the trial you face. We must have a relationship with Jesus Christ. Jesus is waiting with opened arms to carry it for you and take the pain away. He will relieve you of your helplessness, your burden, and help you smile again. God wants to make a soldier out of you, a soldier for the army of the Lord. Jesus will meet that need. Give God a try. I was about to lose my mind, and found out that I wasn't alone.

There are a lot of miserable people who don't have to be, but don't know how to get free. The pain that I had may be different than yours, but it's the same God that will wipe away the tears.

The Deliverance

When I came back to the Lord, I had a lot of baggage. God allowed me to dump the whole load on Him. I was free from fear in my heart, mind, and inner being. Depression left, sadness went away, and pain and misery soon followed. I was able to think clearly, see things differently, and focus my attention on that which loves me the most. Jesus is the one that took away my cares of the world, and showed me that I am someone. Each day I pray and have fellowship with the Lord and others who love Him. I put my effort toward the things of God; as a result, I became absorbed in His goodness, His grace, and His peace that passeth all understanding. I didn't realize that the love that I so desperately needed was right there in front of me. That love that I needed to recover and return to sanity. You can go to God right now, you don't have to wait until tragedy strikes. Seek Him while you're rich in laughter, while your joy is full, and while He may be found. I am talking to you, that someone who has, had, or still is facing some of the same bitter episodes in your own life. Not some mediocre problem (a flat tire), I'm talking about the big one, the problem that turned your whole world around. You, the one who is ashamed of who you are, or what you have become. You, who tried everything and still don't know what to do. You, the person who gave up long time ago, and time and time again you're faced with the same issues. You, the one who fell in love with the person that broke your heart. You, the one who's faced with challenges that try to break, destroy, and ruin your life I'm talking to you. The one that sunk into depression, the one that turned to drugs, and the one that thought they had life all figured out, God got it! Your deliverance is in the hands of Jesus. He helps me every day, and He will help you. I write this book to tell you of my struggle and my breakthrough. Maybe there is someone who can take my heartache as an example that you can make it. Take it as a sign, a miracle, and as a tool until your deliverance unfolds. I needed to give up something that I loved, like God gave up something that He loves—His son, Jesus. Therefore, I pray, take communion, and sometimes fast for my deliverance. You can make it because I made it and I was torn up, real torn, beneath the veil.

PAMELA L. ELLIS

The Growth

When I was able to accept myself, I began to wonder why I so broken. Lord, why did you forsake me? This was my cry to the Lord as if it was His fault, as if He should have magically made the scars disappear, literally. I knew that He could, but would He? After the years went by I quickly learned, no, God is not a magician, He wouldn't remove it magically, but He would help me get through it. He doesn't promote tragedies, and certainly doesn't place stumbling blocks in our paths to harm us; it's not His motive. Little did I know that help was on the way, and that my prayers were not going up in vain. He would bring me to a level in Him so that I could get past it; He would allow me the opportunity to lift Him up. He would keep me that I may share my testimonies with others, that they may take some of these same steps to get their breakthrough. When we need help God will give us everything that we need, and some of the things that we ask for. Oh the things that God has prepared for those that love the Lord. I will be all that God made me to be. I will do all that God has instructed me to do, not because I say so, not because somebody else says so, but because God said so. His word shall not return unto Him void (Isaiah 55:11). The one thing that you could never get rid of will leave. It could take three days, thirty days, or thirty years, but God can get rid of it. I wish above measure that you would prosper and be in good health (III John 2). Good health includes a healthy mind, your mind reflects your thinking, your thinking reflects your actions, and your actions reflects your character. It all begins with godly thinking, get your mind right and so shall you prosper.

There are three steps to a healthy mind:

1. Praise and worship, lift up the name of Jesus at all times.
2. Fellowship with God, study and be a doer of the word.
3. Let the Holy Spirit of God lead, guide, and comfort you.

When you put all of these principles in your life the devil can't keep you broken. I didn't say you wouldn't have any problems, because all that live in Christ Jesus will suffer persecution. I'm pointing out that through Christ Jesus you can make it, without Him, it's a bunch of heartache that wasn't made for

REAL TORN... BENEATH THE VEIL

us to handle, alone. If you refuse to apply these steps in your life then you can expect to be torn to pieces. I know it hurts, I know that someone told you that they would help you, and I know that some of you are all alone, but don't quit. I tell you in the name of Jesus that if you wait on the Lord, serve Him with gladness, and stand on His word, He will see you through. Believe what He tells you. Say this small prayer (you don't need a list of fancy words). Lord, teach me to know thy ways, allow me to have the kind of experience with you that makes a difference in my life, that I may be a better steward in Jesus' name, Amen.

Chapter Six

The Breakthrough

    Nobody but Jesus, the author and finisher of my faith, knows my potential. He knew the purpose that He bestowed upon me. He knew that He would make good what the devil meant for bad, and use it for God's glory. I got my breakthrough, as I believed the Lord. He said, "You are My child," He called me "His child," therefore, He is my Father. Now I realize that I am His little girl, and that little girls go to their daddy when they have a problem. He will protect me; after all, He cares for me. I tell you the moment that I got a revelation of what Jesus did for me, an understanding that people may not like me and certainly can't help me. I depended on a relationship with Jesus. Since I was very scorned, I needed more than the laying of human hands on me. I needed something that my husband couldn't give me, and my kids knew nothing about (oh yeah, I got married and had kids). Hallelujah to Jesus, the devil thought he had me. I needed the kind of breakthrough that only God could give, the kind of peace that passes all understanding. What I needed from God was an impartation from the Holy Ghost. Newness, I needed God to look at me, for Jesus to show up and show out on the scene. My scars were not only on my face; they were embedded in my heart. Only God could penetrate the heart; after all, He created it. It's His breath that I breathe each day after he breathed the breath of life in my nostrils. Without Him I had no heartbeat; certainly He could restore what He made. I may be speaking to someone that is still heartbroken. Maybe you're in a mess, broke, confused, tormented, and abused. Whatever your walk of life, whatever life has dealt to you, there is a way out. Don't panic, don't wait, just give it to God. I need to look like what I look like, to get God's message across to those who have a greater need, those of you that have a secret that you may not want to reveal. You may be a millionaire and miserable, you're not broke but broken. God got it; you can give that problem to the Lord. You see, money can't by your happiness, and surgery can't fix it either. You say, "Oh yes it can." Well let me ask you this, "Are you happy, are you missing something in your life, have you absolutely everything that you need?" If you've answered yes to at least one of these questions, you need Jesus in your life. Since this change has come over me, I am so excited to share my story to help you get through what you're going through. May God use me for His particular glory.

I'm Free

The moment that I realized that the Lord had the power to set me free, I became free. To say what God told me to say, and to be who God told me to be. I became free to take the headbands off, and pull the bangs back. I am free because Jesus set me free. And whom the Lord sets free is free indeed (John 8:36). I have never been so happy, never was I so confident. It could not be done without the Lord on my side. I know what it means to be free, no traps. I recall Dr. Leroy Thompson saying, "No more limits, no more boundaries." I am safe, secure, and free because Jesus died for me. Therefore, you are no longer a slave but a son, and if a son, then a heir of God through Christ (Galatians 4:7). I've been set free by the Lord God almighty, and Jesus Christ our Lord. He broke the chains, loosed the shackles, and set me free. He alone took my pain away; He kept me from falling when I couldn't keep myself. I want to encourage you, that whatever your load, dilemma, or captivity. I know a God that can move mountains. God, who is rich in mercy, full of grace that sits high and looks low. There is nothing hidden from His sight. He sees all things that go on in our lives, and there is nothing hidden that shall not be revealed. He is able to lift you up when you're down, and place your feet on higher ground. I am lifted up; you therefore, be ye lifted up. I shall call on the name of the Lord forever; I'll sing Him praises and bless His holy name. In the day of trouble He shall hide me and will hide you Come on, help me bless His mighty name. I am to walk in the pleasures of life, I am able to cross the bridge to the other side, and hold my head high without shame or weariness. Christ Jesus strengthens me; it is when I am weak that He is made strong. You may be saying, "Pam, that is not easy to do," then I'll say, "No, it isn't, but you can believe what God said to you, about you." Give it to Jesus, He knows all about it, He may not come when you want Him, but He will be there right on time. It is not about me, it's about a savior ready to take the pain away, a savior that wants to set you free, too. It's never too late, I thought my life was over; but I'm still here bound free. There is therefore now no more condemnation for those who are in Christ Jesus, who do not walk according to the flesh, but according to the Spirit (Romans 8:1).

My Father's Business

Over the years, God has shown me that He is with me. He showed me that His mighty hand controls my life. I could hear God's calling in ways that I would never forget. I heard the Lord say "Preach," on numerous occasions and I know that His word would not return unto Him void (Isaiah 55:11). Preaching is a job done by those who are called of the One and only true God, the God of the Bible. "The Spirit of the Lord is upon me, because He has anointed me to preach the gospel to the poor; He has sent me to heal the brokenhearted, to proclaim liberty to the captives, and recovery of sight to the blind. To set at liberty those who are oppressed; To proclaim the acceptable year of the Lord," (Luke 4:18). Preach to the people that they too may be set free from the snares of the devil. To remove bondage and strongholds, to rebuke, encourage, exhort, and deliver souls from the clutches of Satan. My God has spoken to me with a message that He will help me, He will guide me, and all that I have to do is trust Him. He said, "Don't worry. Just trust me." I can trust in the almighty God to do that in which He said He would do. I can stand on His promises and trust in His word. He will rebuke the devourer for my sake and yours. To boldly go where the Holy Spirit leads, my God shall go with me along the way. Now, I don't want you to take this lightly, I certainly do not; it's powerful when the Lord shows up and speaks to you. It's unlike any other voice in the history of this world. No one can imitate, no one can mock Him, and no one can take His place. I tell you that the Holy Ghost of God is awesome in every endeavor. He created a foundation that can never be broken, a kingdom that cannot be removed, and raised a standard that cannot be shaken. God has shown me only a portion of His marvelous hand when He shook my ceiling twice, and said, "There is nothing hidden from My sight." I thought that I was in a dream, oh but it was real. He filled my living room with power that was so huge, I thought that I was about to leave this place. He filled me with his Holy Spirit with the evidence of speaking in tongues, He loosed the shackles and set me free, and my God shall never leave me. He put down in me what no one can take away, and anoints my head with oil almost every day. Now I am not boasting, but lifting Him up, for He is worthy of honor, testimonies and praise. For I am thankful to Him and bless His name, for the Lord He is God, and we are His people.

Chapter Seven

At Forty-Two

I'm older now, with a little more knowledge than before and filled with the Spirit of God. Today I pray that the enemy that has camped around you be defeated. I want to encourage you to be all that you are called to be. Today, I am on a mission to help someone else get free, to meet the need of people with the word of God, and to help someone step out into his or her very own potential. It's almost like striking it rich and going back to the community to share the wealth, but better. I can tell you this, in the name of Jesus, I had to go through something to tell someone else how to overcome. Personally speaking, I can't learn much from a person with no experience. I had to be taught by the master, the creator, and the motivator. The Holy Ghost of God stepped into my situation and showed me His power. All that I needed was a touch from God to get my mind right. I had to learn how to give it all to Jesus, and stand on His word. To listen to Him when He speaks to me, to do what He says to do, and to be who He said I would be. To give Him my troubles and leave them there, to walk boldly in the shadow of His might. There is no issue that He can't fix, and no circumstance that He can't handle. The most important thing to remember is that Jesus Christ is Lord, and He will do what He said He would do. Doesn't matter if it's twenty-six years or twenty-six minutes, wait on the Lord. I gave up, gave in, and threw in the towel, but my Lord never left or forsook me. He waited until I was ready and allowed me to return back into His loving arms. He is the perfect gentleman, He won't force us to do anything, and He loves us just as we are. So the next time you think that you can't go on, think again, you can make it. If you got to scrawl to the cross keep scrawling, eventually you'll make it across the highest mountain. Be strong in the Lord, and in the power of His might (Ephesians 6:10).

New Beginnings

Lord, You changed in me that which was necessary to change. You caused me to like myself and love who You have allowed me to become. You have prepared me every step of the way, and have given me the words to say. You have allowed me to pray for, talk to, and encourage the people. You hold the master plan and the secret of life in your hands. When I sought You with my whole heart, You allowed me to find You. You told me, "Don't worry, brace yourself, press your way, I'm pressing you!" Lord, I thank You. Thank You for waiting patiently for me, for allowing me to return unto You. For restoring in me that which was broken, that which was destroyed, and that which was real torn. Oh I see this change that has come over me, it causes me to press on towards the mark of the higher calling. Press on when things go right, when things go wrong, and when things are not at all my way. To get over the mistakes of yesterday, and get ready for Your promises of today. God got it, a new season with brand new blessings and brand new people. A new beginning, yes, that requires a fresh start and the opening up of a door that had been shut. Today is the day that the Lord has made and I will rejoice and be glad in it (Psalms 118:24). To hold fast to His unchanging hands and know that His word shall do that in which He instructed. Oh the Spirit of the Living God falls fresh upon me, it satisfies my heart, my mind and my soul. This brand new start causes me to cry out to God for which cometh my help. "Thank You, Jesus!" This is another day that the Lord has made, seemingly brighter than the last one. This day has brand new meanings and brand new mercies; this time is quite different than the previous. New beginnings, that which was predestined before my time, that which was established without my help. The beginning of what was already planned, that which I had not arranged, a new beginning. God got me; He has set the stage for my appointed time to preach. He will help me and guide me that I am ready at His command. God has bestowed in me His powerful seal of the Holy Ghost (II Corinthians 1:22) and (Ephesians 4:30), that which authenticates ownership. Allowing me to understand a glimpse of His love and His will. To receive His calling that He continues to reassure in me. He is my father, my friend, my fortress, and my rock. He is preparing me to do His will, and corrects me gently when I am impatient; He causes me to know that He holds everything together in the palms of his hands. It is only because of His mercy that I have a brand new beginning.

The Work

The work is not easy; you can't just walk in front of people and start talking about God; it takes an anointing from the Holy Ghost. Ministry requires a relationship with Jesus. Almost anyone can give a presentation; some people are good at talking a lot with big fancy words. But is it life changing; will people be saved, set free and delivered? Do they come out from under their influence with a hope of the coming Messiah? Jesus, He is the author and finisher of our faith. Through prayer, encouragement, and a listening ear people are redirected to the love of Christ. Can you honestly say that you've allowed Him to change your life? He chose me as His vessel (many are called but few chosen), as a living witness of what the Lord can do. Not by Power, not by might, but by My Spirit says the Lord (Zechariah 4:6). I have to remain humble to be used of God so that He can meet the needs of His people. It's a challenge that only God can prepare me for. Preach the word! Be ready in season and out of season. Convince, rebuke, exhort, with all longsuffering and teaching (2 Timothy 4:2). He prepares me simply because people cannot or will not always want to hear the truth. For the time will come when they will not endure sound doctrine, but according to their own desires, because they have itching ears, they will heap up for themselves teachers; and they will turn their ears away from the truth, and be turned aside to fables (2 Timothy 4:3,4). God that wishes none would perish but come into the knowledge of His truth uses people like you and I to take the gospel to the nations. As the days go by I see miracles unfolding, the blessings falling down, and people crying out for a new day and a breakthrough in their lives. As for me, there is no turnaround. I can't imagine life without the Lord on my side. I love you, people, and pray for you all; after all, Jesus died for the people. Although I minister to you, I minister to myself. Every so often I have to turn off the television, turn off the telephone, and get in the presence of the Lord. He has to fill my cup so that I can pour into His people once again. The work requires that I listen to the Holy Spirit of God and follow His lead. No matter the situation, the circumstance or what someone else says, my instruction comes from above. There are some people who think that I should listen to them, and their intentions may be good, but if it doesn't line up with the "word" and what the Lord has spoken to me, it doesn't matter. If God were not able to feed me, direct me, and keep me, then I certainly wouldn't need anyone else. I serve a God that is able to do it, He will keep me, He will feed me, and He will fill my cup, or else all my work is in vain. I heard the Holy Ghost say, "It ain't in vain!"

P.A.S.S.I.O.N:
Power & Atonement for Suffering, Sin, and Iniquities in Our Nation/ Monthly Sermons for Daily Life

January 2007/Peace

Beloved, do not think it strange concerning the fiery trial which is to try you, as though some strange thing happened to you (1 Peter 4:12). When things go wrong we say, "Why has this happened? I did everything that I was supposed to do, I've been fair, nice, and I am a good person. What have I done to deserve this?" We believe that problems should not occur against us—maybe someone else—but not to us. As though some strange thing has happened, we cannot believe that problems has aroused in our life. Some of us think that we're all alone, that problems only happens to us and no one else, as if others never have any trouble. Whatever our thoughts, we are not alone (we're supposed to go through); it's the testing of our faith. Life is full of tests, we will have trials, we will be tried, God will try us, and the enemy will throw the darts. How much will we endure? God wants to know, what will we do in the mist of trouble, what will we put up with. Will we go the extra mile, for the joy that has been set before us? Some of us say that we will, but when things happen, we wonder, "Why, has God allowed this to happen to me?" We say, "God has the authority to change this situation, why hasn't He taken the pain away?" Yes, God does have the capability. He can take it away, but doesn't always remove it. In the Garden of Gethsemane, Jesus, was going through an emotional ordeal. He was going to be crucified on the cross for us. He prayed about it, and asked the Father (God), to remove that ultimate sacrifice, that burden of pain, to change the course. He thought about the load, the heaviness of it, about what he had to do. After He sought the Father, Jesus spoke saying, "Nevertheless, not my will, but thy will be done," (Matthew 26:36-39). In that moment, He demonstrated his love for the Father. He proved that He wanted to please the Father, to please Him in everyway. He wanted to let God know that whatever happened, to God be the glory. For this reason, we know that God doesn't always come and take us out of the situation, but helps us get through it. I know, we don't want to go through anything, we want to be comfortable all of our life. But life isn't always comfortable for us, and may not be that easy either; but we can make it. God wants to see what we'll do in the mist of our trouble, and trouble will come. God is still on the throne, the devil is alive and real. Your adversary the devil walks about like a roaring lion, seeking whom he may devour (1 Peter 5:8). It's his job to try to destroy us. It's his job to steal our joy. But what are we going to do about it? You ask, "What can we do?" I'll tell you. Open the Bible, turn to Ephesians 5:14,15,16,17. We can put on the breastplate of righteousness, the helmet of salvation, and the shield of faith. The word of God (The Holy Bible), will guide us into the truth and knowledge of Jesus Christ. There is a way of escape for the trial we face, we do not have to face it alone. God may not come when we want him, but He will be right there on time. Those that come to God must know that he is God, and that he is a rewarder of those that diligently seek him (Heb. 11:6). The only requirement is that we believe in the One that can keep us in perfect peace.

February 2007/The Woman at the Well

A woman of Samaria came to draw water. Jesus said to her, "Give Me a drink." Then the woman of Samaria said to Him, "How is it that You, being a Jew, ask a drink from me, a Samaritan woman?" (John 4:9). Jesus answered and said to her, "If you knew the gift of God, and who it is who says to you, 'Give Me a drink,' you would have asked Him, and He would have given you living water." (John 4:10). Isn't it something when people say that they know God, but when He speaks to them, they don't know that its Him. When you are familiar with someone you become accustomed to their voice. Jesus said, "My sheep know my voice" (John 10:27). It is apparent that this woman was not one of His sheep, not of His fold, and set apart from those that belong to Him. She said, "I know that the messiah is coming (who is called Christ), when He comes, He will tell us all things." Jesus said, "I who speak to you am He." Had she been a follower of Jesus (a Christian), already, she would have known that this Man that spoke with her was indeed the Lord. She heard someone say that Christ is coming, maybe truly believed it, but didn't know Him for herself. It's not enough to believe what someone says about Jesus, you must know Him for yourself. She had not a real relationship with God, for if she had known the Father (God), certainly, she would have known the Son (Jesus), That all should honor the Son just as they honor the Father. He who does not honor the Son does not honor the Father who sent Him (John 5:23). The woman left her water pot, went her way into the city, and said to the men, "Come, see a Man who told me all things that I ever did. Could this be the Christ?" Therefore, she was not sure, yet. When the Lord stands before you and speaks, there will be no uncertainty, no doubt, no mistake. You will know that you're in the presence of the Lord. You won't be confused (trembling a bit), but not confused, you will know that it's Him. As we all know, we were born of the flesh (from our mother's womb). That which is born of flesh is flesh and that which is born of Spirit is spirit. You must be born again, not by the womb of your mother, again, but by the Holy Spirit of God. This woman had not worshipped the Lord in spirit and truth, for God is spirit, for those that worship Him must worship Him in spirit and truth (John 4:24). Ask God for the new birth that only comes from Him through Jesus Christ that you may be able to worship Him in spirit and truth. When the Lord comes you may recognize Him that can save you. When you pray, expect results, know who it is that you're praying to. Many of the Samaritans of that city believed in Him because of the word of the woman who testified, "He told me all that I ever did." So when the Samaritans had come to Him, they urged Him to stay with them; and He stayed there two days. And many more believed because of His own word. Then they said to the woman, "Now we believe, not because of what you said, for we ourselves have heard Him and we know that this is indeed the Christ, the Savior of the world." Jesus said, "Most assuredly, I say to you, unless one is born again, he cannot see the kingdom of God (John 3:3).

March 2007/The Truth Shall Make You Free

All too often, we settle for words that are not true. To help us feel good, we accept what doesn't hurt, we would rather believe a lie. When we believe something that is not true, we're unable to face reality. Little do we know, that in order to receive one lie, we must retrieve another. As a result, we become bound by lies, and overcome with grief all because we didn't believe the truth. But, when we believe the truth and face what we didn't want to see, we become free. In order for you to be free you must know the truth. Jesus will set you free. Therefore, if the Son makes you free, you're free indeed (John 8:36). The God of the Bible doesn't operate with a bunch of lies. God is the father of truth, He will set you free from bondage. The devil is the father of lies (John 8:44), he wants you to believe that you're a nobody. Let me explain. Every time we believe that we're hopeless and a waste of life, that is a lie. Every time we believe what others say about us (she'll never amount to anything) that is a lie. A lie is the untold truth, something that we are accustomed to believe, it has become more than what most of us call, "a little white lie." The opposite of the truth is a lie, either you believe one or the other. Webster describes *truth* as a: the pathway to freedom, b: the quality or state of being true. It describes a lie as a: something that is not true, b: falsified information, c: it only leads to bondage and captivity. Jesus said, "If you abide in My word, you are My disciples indeed, and you shall know the truth and the truth shall make you free" (John 8:32). There is no way that you can experience freedom until you believe the truth. There was a woman in the Bible with an issue of blood for twelve years (Matt 9:20-22). She believed that she would not stop bleeding, she was bound by what was going on in her life (after all what else should she believe—but that which she could see) the devil thought he had her for life, that was a lie. Jesus made her well the moment that she believed that He could. There also was a woman with an infirmity that had her bent over for eighteen years (Luke 13:11, 12). Imagine, for all of those years, she believed that she could never stand again, she believed a lie. Jesus saw her and said, "Woman thou art loosed from your infirmity," immediately she was set free and made whole, because she believed Jesus (the truth). You can be made whole at precisely the moment that you believe, a burden will be lifted off, instantaneously, you will become free, free to believe the truth. Right now you have know idea that you're trapped in a web of lies, you are blindfolded with scales on your eyes. You can't see that the enemy has encamped around you. But God can set you free, free from that which has kept you bound. Free from the depths of hell and torment for the rest of your life. Believe that God can change your circumstance, believe that Jesus died on the cross to set you free.

Believe that one day (no man knows the hour), Jesus will return with His mighty angels to take those that are His away to glory. Believe that! I assure you that once you believe, the scales will fall away from your eyes. The devil thought he had me. I too, believed God, received the truth, and became free.

April 2007/The Holy Ghost

For there are three that bear witness in Heaven: The Father, the Word, and the Holy Spirit and these three are one. And there are three that bear witness on earth: the Spirit, the water, and the blood; and these three agree as one (I John 5:7,8). God the Father is creator of everything; Jesus is the Word that became flesh, the savior of the world, and the Holy Ghost is the Spirit of the living God. Now, the Holy Spirit is the comforter that the Father will send in Jesus' name, to teach us all things, and to bring all things to our remembrance, whatsoever Jesus has said unto us (John 14:26). When the Holy Spirit comes upon you, you will receive power (Acts 1:8). He will come in the midnight hour, the noonday, or at any other time to speak the truth (He cannot tell a lie). He will lead you and guide you in the midst of any trouble and make a way of escape for you. The comforter, which is the Holy Ghost, will stir your spirit up and prepare you for the holiness of God. The Holy Ghost of God will keep your heart, and mind, through Christ Jesus. He will minister to your heart and prepare you for your destiny with the Lord. He will call you by name, and you will stop in your tracks to collect your thoughts. He will call you out of darkness into His marvelous light. He will quicken your spirit and speak to you in the midst of the darkest secret in your life. Someone asked me, "What do you mean God speaks to you?" I said, "He speaks, He spoke to me just as plain as I am speaking to you. So the next time that you hear that voice saying, 'That is not right,' or 'Don't do that,' you won't say, 'Something told me,' when you serve the Lord, the voice that you hear is the Holy Spirit of God. The Holy Spirit will reveal to you the things that satisfy deep down in your soul." The Holy Spirit will speak to you (Acts 28:25). Gives gifts (1 Corinthians 12:3-11). Helps in our weaknesses (Romans 8:26). Guides (John 16:13). Baptizes (Acts 2:17-41). Anoints (1 John 2:20). Convicts Men (John 16:8-11). Renews (Isaiah 32:15). Gives discernment (1 Corinthians 2:10-16). Fills (Acts 2:4). Comforts (Acts 9:31). The Holy Ghost will teach you how to pray, for we no not what we ought to pray (Romans 8:26). For if you live according to the flesh you will die, but if by the Spirit you put to death the deeds of the body, you will live. For as many as are led by the Spirit of God, these are sons of God. The Spirit Himself bears witness with our spirit that we are children of God, and if children we are also heirs (Romans 8:13-17).

May 2007/Persecuted

I heard this choir sing this song; I believe that it is called "Praise Your Way Out." It goes something like this. Persecuted so heavy laden, cast down, right on your face. You've been feeling that you can't go on, and it seems that you're just about to lose your mind. The thing about it gets really next to you, you just don't understand why you're going through it. Say hallelujah, say thank you Jesus, say hallelujah, say thank you Jesus, praise your way out. That song ministers to the heart of those who are going through a bitter time in life. Its purpose is to identify how you're feeling, and what steps to take to get you through what it is that you're going through. Bless those that persecute you: bless and do not curse (Romans 12:14). I know that it's hard to love people that don't love you back. I realize that it is difficult to be friendly to the unfriendly, but the Bible says to do it. We must bite our tongues; glue our mouths shut, or tape them closed. Whatever is necessary for us to do what the word of God says to do. The anointing costs much; you may have give up some stuff, your old way of doing things, the bad habits and the ungodly thinking. We're going to go through persecution before we get to the kingdom of heaven. Oh, but it will be well worth it on the other side when we sit down at Jesus' feet. No more cares of this present world, no more problems and people taking advantage of our goodness because we're lovers of Jesus. It really isn't the fault of people, for their blinded by the enemy of this world. It's a set up; they've been set up to try to destroy us before we get there. The apostle Paul was used to persecuting Christians, the scripture reads as follows. And I thank Christ Jesus our Lord who has enabled me because He counted me faithful, putting me into the ministry, although I was formerly a blasphemer, a persecutor, and an insolent man; but I obtained mercy because I did it ignorantly in unbelief (1 Timothy 1: 12, 13). Satan binds anyone who is not redeemed by Christ; there is no way around it. Persecution is an experience for all of us to go through because Jesus went through, the only difference, is that it's worst when you're not walking with the Lord. Jesus said, "Remember the word that I said to you, 'A servant is not greater than his master.' If they persecuted Me, they will also persecute you" (John 15:20). They persecuted Him first and Jesus sits at the right hand of God. Therefore, Jesus said, " Blessed are you when they revile and persecute you, and say all kinds of evil against you falsely for My sake. Rejoice and be exceedingly glad, for great is your reward in heaven, for so they persecuted the prophets who were before you." The word of God says, We are persecuted but not forsaken; struck down, but not destroyed (II Corinthians 4:9). Therefore, though we are abused, broken, and real torn we are not forgotten. The day shall come when we will reign with Christ.

June 2007/The Waiting Game

Those that wait upon the Lord shall renew their strength; they shall mount up with wings as eagles, they shall run and not be weary, they shall walk and not faint (Isaiah 40: 31).

For some of us waiting is one of the hardest things to do. We realize that the promise is coming, we know that God said it would, but how long? When is it going to happen, when is the change going to come, when can I expect the new arrival? We wonder, *What is going to happen tomorrow, what can we do to make the process progress?* We may be waiting on God for months, or years, but if God said so, you better believe it. You may have to tell yourself, self, we're going to believe God, and we're going to act like it. I know it's hard waiting on that thing that God promised you, but keep doing what He told you to do. You don't have to go to God and beg, He heard you the first time. The waiting requires for you to listen for the next step, the next move, and get ready; it's coming. It's a process; some things that God did in 20 minutes for others may take 20 days for you. But there is something that you can do while you're waiting. Read the word, get in right standing with the Lord, make sure you're living right, do what the word says to do. Seek God's face in prayer; don't go to sleep in your anger. It's like a woman in labor, she knows that eventually she's going to have that baby. For she knows that in a certain amount of time the baby will be due. It doesn't matter how long it takes, that baby will arrive, and so, the waiting game begins. The woman prepares for and waits on the new arrival. But in the meantime, she feeds that baby, exercises, and gets enough rest so that baby will be healthy, not immature. We as people get in a hurry; we want everything right now. Wait on the Lord, His timing is right and He makes no mistakes. To everything there is a season, a time for every purpose under heaven: A time to be born, and a time to die; a time to plant, and a time to pluck what is planted; a time to kill, and a time to heal; a time to break down, and a time to build up; a time to weep, and a time to laugh; a time to mourn, and a time to dance; a time to cast away stones, and a time to gather stones; a time to embrace, and a time to refrain from embracing; a time to gain, and a time to lose; a time to keep, and a time to throw away; a time to tear, and a time to sew; a time to keep silence, and a time to speak; a time to love, and a time to hate; a time of war, and a time of peace (Ecclesiastes 3:1-8). God is preparing you. He knows when the time is right for you; don't be discouraged. He can't put you out there and give you a million bucks—you'd lose your mind. He has to prepare you. Wait for the Lord to set it up; it's a process. God will use people that you never thought imaginable to bless you. He will set things up so that you would know that it was nobody but Him. The blessing is better when it takes awhile to get it. You will appreciate it more and won't take it for granted. Therefore, when the waiting is over, you'll be happy you waited. Amen.

July 2007/Hold On

Brethren, I do not count myself to have apprehended, but one thing I do, forgetting those things which are behind and reaching forward to those things which are ahead, I press toward the goal for the prize of the upward call of God in Christ Jesus (Philippians 3:13,14). Today is a new day, the day in which former things have passed away. We can walk in the newness, the newness that God has bestowed upon us. It's okay to get excited about new things that have been done in our lives. Walking upright with God, doing all that He has us to do, focusing our attention on the things above and not of this world. There is a higher calling that calls for us to live holy and make sacrifices unto our God. To be right in His sight for there is nothing hidden that shall not be revealed. We ought to live respectably before God, fearing Him that made us. Thus, it is written that one day we will meet our maker, we will be with the Lord. We are accountable for what has been given us, to share in the teaching of the gospel. Don't worry about what someone says about you, worry about what God said. Therefore, I encourage you to hold on to what has been given you, let no one take it away. I tell you that no man gave it, and no man can take it away. Hold firm hands to what you believe and the things that you've been entrusted with. The power of God that lives deep down in your spirit cannot be moved or shaken. Hallelujah to Jesus; let the Spirit of God walk with you and listen to His direction. Don't move to the right, and don't move to the left, hold on to the promise. I tell you, what you got in your possession is what the angel's desire (1 Peter 1:12). Press on and be strong, hold on and do not lose heart, hold to your faith, and hold on to His love. Our maker will not delay, but arrive, just as He said He would. I know that you've been waiting and waiting and nothing happened, but wait a little longer. God isn't through with you yet. From the looks of it, you may think that He has forgotten you. No worries, He hasn't forgot about you; your soul is too precious, His love is too strong, and the word of God is a lamp to your feet and a light unto your pathway (Psalm 119:105). You've been called hold on to your calling, let the power that lives in thee keep thee, you've been called to holiness. In Jesus' name hold on to it.

August 2007/Do It for Jesus

For those who know to do right and does not do it, to him it is sin (James 4:17). Life is so full of temptations that it is hard to let go of sin. We've all been there and some of us still are. We make excuses for the reason why we don't change, and get upset when someone loves us enough to warn us. Change is good, and especially to make your life in agreement with the Lord, the change that will make a difference and some day present you before God in heaven. There is no temptation that can overcome us; we don't have to give in to sin. God will not give us more than we can handle. I've been faced with some difficult moments in my life, but the result is that I can stand before you and say I have been changed. I am being prepared daily for that difficult moment, the temptation that stares me in the face. That temptation that knocks on my door, begging me to let it in, I got to rebuke it. I've got to say, "In the name of Jesus, get thee behind me, Satan." If you can't do it because it's the right thing to do, if you can't do it for yourselves, do it for Jesus. Jesus, Him that knew no sin, died in our place that we might have life. Jesus, that loves us more than we love our selves, He went to the cross for you and I, that we may escape the fiery flames. Though He was tempted beyond measure He overcame and gave know way to the devil. There is a way made for us the Bible says, "Resist the devil and he will flee from you" (James 4:7). The devil has to flee, but you have to resist him. You have to resist the thought, the memory, and that thing that makes you fall into temptation. Whatever it is, if it causes you to fall, get rid of it. Finally, brethren, whatever things are true, whatever things are noble, whatever things are just, whatever things are pure, whatever things are lovely, whatever things are of good report, if there is any virtue and if there is anything praise worthy meditate on these things (Philippians 4:8). Live your life right, to the fullness of the Lord, do what He desires for you to do. Whatever pleases the Father is what the Son does. We, too, as children of God should be willing to do that in which the Father will honor. Do it for Jesus.

September 2007/Expectations

Every time we expect someone to do something for us, we hold that person accountable, and we're disappointed when they don't come through for us. Now we're upset and never want to speak to that person again; all because they weren't able to hold up to their end of our plan. Everyone is mad except the devil, because now he has his expectations met. He expected you to do exactly what you did. He likes it when we get upset with each other so we won't build each other up. If we stop expecting people to do things for us we won't get our feeling hurt, and be equipped to serve a mighty God. How many of us know that when we serve a mighty God (the one that is rich in mercy and owns the cattle on a thousand hills) we don't have a need that can't be met? When we live according to the word of God, we receive the full benefits of the kingdom; therefore, we can expect a harvest, a miracle and a breakthrough. Some of us have our expectations in the wrong places, then when things go wrong, and they will, we fall out with each other. Therefore, you also be ready, for the Son of Man is coming at an hour you do not expect (Luke 12:40). Keep your expectations on Jesus; therefore, you can expect to reign with Christ, expect to be blessed, expect to be changed. Stop obligating folks; it's not up to them to take care of you, or take you to heaven. Since you know that you're walking upright with the Lord, you can expect Him to meet your every need.

You could rely on Jesus and depend on His promises, because Jesus won't disappoint. Some of the things that we asked for we didn't need anyhow. Be careful for what you ask for because you might get it, then become overwhelmed and burden when you do. Change your priorities, get your expectations right, focus on the one that you can expect to treat you right. Once you get a revelation of Him (whom you should be expecting), you will live your life accordingly. You can expect to be changed and ready in that unexpected hour.

October 2007/I Am Watching You

There is an unction from the Holy Ghost, that causes you to move when God says, "Move." You can't sit still, your spirit can't rest, and you have to go until the assignment is complete. In the same token, there are certain things that you will do when God says, "I'm watching you." You will think about it, and it will be on your mind for days maybe even months. You'll never forget that one sentence; it will last you a lifetime. Have you ever been frozen, afraid to move, or too scared to look? That is the way it feels when God shows up. It's like you're afraid to breathe, because your heart may make a sudden unscheduled sound, an unwanted sound. In that moment, you want nothing but silence, you want to be certain that you get all that God came to give you. In that moment, you hope that God is pleased with you and would like for Him to tell you just that. Although you're afraid, you want absolutely everything, every question answered and every need met. I know it's scary when God shows up, He is bigger than anything you could ever imagine. And because we can't see Him (John 1:18), He gets our uttermost, undivided attention. His presence makes our whole world stop, everything is of little importance. Things that used to matter to you don't matter anymore, all that we've focused our attention on doesn't mean a thing. I'm watching you, it could mean to stand still, don't go over there; but stay right here. I heard the Lord say, "I'm watching you." It's not like being on the job when the boss comes we straighten up, because we know that she is on the way. I am talking about a God that sees all things, that know all things, and there is nothing hidden from His sight. When God is watching you, you're careful to live right, to talk right, and to honor Him by walking in His counsel. You keep an eye out for God by doing what He says to do, you pray, and study the word seeking His face. God will do in your life what He said He would do. I don't care what it looks like, move under the direction of the Holy Ghost, don't go looking for a sign, or for someone to take you there, wait on the Lord to tell you when to move, He will release you when you're ready. I know that I am being watched, so it causes me to want to be pleasing in His sight. To evaluate myself, correct my attitude, love right, think right, and to pay attention to; and, act on the word of God. To hear His voice when He calls me, when He directs me, and guides me. I'm watching you.

November 2007/God on Your Side

Ever heard the song "Long as I Got King Jesus, I Don't Need Nobody Else"? Well, that is the way that David felt when he fought with Goliath. He knew that the Lord was on his side; therefore, he had not worried what the giant could do. David believed God that He would not leave him in the midst of his circumstance, in the midst of his trial, or even in the midst of his trouble. There is something about God's ability of when we trust Him. He begins to perform His word to do that in which He instructed it to do (Isaiah 55:11). David knew that God said to trust Him, he knew that whatever means necessary God would not let Him down. David was aware that although Goliath was big in size, God is even bigger. David knew that although the circumstance looked grim, things are not all that they appear to be. Therefore, he trusted in God, that God would be right there on his side, that the ball was in David's court, that the man that appeared to be strong wasn't so strong after all. Have you ever experienced God on your side? Have you ever had a situation that made you wonder, *How in the world did I get through that?* Did you ever stop to think, *Why am I still here?* That was God on your side. The same God (the God of the Bible), that saved your soul. That same God, that kept you when you couldn't keep yourself. God was on your side but at the time you didn't know it; you hadn't realized that He was in the midst of your dilemma carrying you, and holding you up. That when you were dead in your sins, God came and lifted you up and pulled you out of the darkness, into His marvelous light. God was on your side. Nobody but Jesus, in the midst of your trial can help you. "Long as you got King Jesus, you don't need nobody else."

PAMELA L. ELLIS

December 2007/It Came upon a Midnight Hour

For unto you is born this day in the city of David a Savior, which is Christ the Lord (Luke 2:11). Isn't it lovely, to know that the Lord is on our side? Thank God for Jesus that He keeps us and would never leave us. In that midnight hour, we have time to think about the pressures of life and how we've been used, abused, mistreated, betrayed and confused. If it were not for Jesus, some of us would have lost our minds long time ago. Those long dark nights that seemed like forever, when morning seems as though it would never show its light. In the midnight hour when all hell breaks loose, the devil told you, "This is it. You won't last until tomorrow, it's over." That same night you believed that God had left you, and that you were hopeless. The night that you started to wonder if there is really a God. If there is truly a God in heaven why doesn't He come and see about me, why would He leave me in this mess? I write this book to tell you that if it had not been for Jesus, we wouldn't have made it through some of those nights. We ought to be thankful that God so loved the world that He gave His only begotten son that whosoever believe in Him shall not perish, but have everlasting life (John 3:16). When it comes upon a midnight hour, we become afraid and defeated. That midnight night hour is able to perform that in which it wants to do, the devil had a trap set. He wanted to keep us so far down in our troubles that we wouldn't notice that there is a light at the end of the tunnel. That there is a lifeguard on duty and our needs will be met. For unto us a child is born, unto us a son is given; and the government shall be upon his shoulder: and his name shall be called Wonderful, Counselor, the Mighty God, the Everlasting Father, the Prince of Peace (Isaiah 9:6). Now, the next time that you come to the sign that reads, "The Midnight Hour," it only comes to remind you of your past and to tell you that you'll always be alone. But don't get discouraged; tell the devil he is a liar and the father thereof (John 8:44). You don't have to have restless nights and gloomy days, pray to Jesus our Savior; He is the one that died to set you and your mind free. In that midnight hour you can rest assured that this too shall pass. Everything in your life has to have a past; yesterday is a day of the past. Your last relationship is of the past; your old job is in the past. The problem that you continue to think about is in the past. Let go and let God. Thank Him that He made a way for us. You may not like all that you are, but you certainly aren't what you used to be (living in the past).

Slowly as the midnight hour approaches, begin to praise God. I guarantee you that morning will come faster than you could ever imagine. You will begin to look forward to the next midnight hour.

Works Cited

Cortier, C The., *Choir, Praise Your Way Out*, audio cassette tape, 1999, Wisconsin.

Jakes, Bishop T.D., Supplemental articles, *Soul Secrets, Leading Ladies, and Gospel Pearls*. Holy Bible, Woman Thou Art Loosed Edition, 1998.

Thompson, Dr. Leroy., *The Abundance Principle*, audio cassette tape, Ever Increasing Word Ministries, Nov. 2001.

To receive monthly newsletters from Pam Ellis Ministry write or call:

PASSION
Pam Ellis Ministry
P.O. Box 3736
LaCrosse, Wi 54602-3736
608 498-1591
Passion.Jesus@hotmail.com
PamEllisministry@charter.net

Please include your prayers, and prayer needs.
God Bless you sister/brother in Christ.

Jesus said, "So the last will be first, and the first last. For many are called, but few chosen," (Matthew 20:16).

The devil thought he had me—scorned, set back, and set up. God said not so! There isn't a challenge in life that God can't help you overcome. He will call you out of darkness into His marvelous light, use you for His glory and love you with all His might. There's "Power!" in the Mighty Matchless name of Jesus.

We will walk the streets of gold after His imminent return. Oh, come on, trust Him, and help me bless His Holy name.

Biography

Pam Ellis is forty-two years old, and the author of *Real Torn... Beneath the Veil*, a true story about a life of pain and struggle. She is also the president of PASSION: Power & Atonement for Suffering, Sin, and Iniquity in Our Nations, an evangelist outreach that reaches out to people through the gospel of Jesus Christ the Lord. She has a biblical diploma from Amazing Facts Bible College and an associate's degree in management. Her wholehearted interest is to preach the gospel nationwide; in addition, she loves to write, roller-skate, and help others in any way that she can. After years of believing that she would never marry, she has been with her husband for twenty-one years; they have three children, ages twenty, sixteen, and four.

Real Torn... Beneath the Veil

Everyone has problems, but what would you do if you were really broken? Would you give up, lose your mind, or crawl back into the hole that you climbed out of?